One in a
Million

Iris Howden

Published in association with
The Basic Skills Agency

Hodder & Stoughton

Cataloguing in Publication Data is available from the British Library.

ISBN 0 340 696958

First published 1997
Impression number   10 9 8 7 6 5 4 3 2 1
Year   2002 2001 2000 1999 1998 1997

Typeset by Fakenham Photosetting Ltd, Fakenham, Norfolk.
Printed in Great Britain for Hodder & Stoughton Educational, a division of
Hodder Headline Plc, 338 Euston Road, London NW1 3BH by Athenaeum Press
Ltd, Gateshead, Tyne & Wear.

One in a Million

Contents

1

Terry

I met Terry Barnes when I was
twelve years old.
His family moved to Burford
from another town,
and Terry came to our school.
The form teacher asked me
to keep an eye on him.
'Sit with Philip,' she told him that first day.
'He'll show you what to do.'

Not that Terry needed much help.
For a new boy he learned fast.

He was soon the leader of our gang.
He made the football team within weeks.
Terry was the sort of kid who always had
the best watch, the newest sports gear,
the bike with the most gears.
He just had to come first.

Terry left school as soon as he was sixteen.
He couldn't wait to start work.
He got a job at once with a firm of builders.
I used to see him in the mornings
waiting for their van to pick him up.
I'd be on my old push bike. He and his mates
would flash past me tooting the horn.
I felt a fool still wearing my school uniform.
I guess I looked a bit of a weed to them.

They were in jeans and T-shirts,

fit and tanned from working all day in the sun.

Soon, Terry was in the driving seat so I knew

he must have passed his test first time.

A couple of years later, when I went to college,
I met up with Terry again.

He was sitting in the canteen drinking coffee.

'Hi, Terry,' I said. 'Are you taking a course?'

'I'm on Day Release,' he told me. 'Bricklaying.
I thought I might as well. You need a proper
qualification to get on in building.'

'Sure. It's great to see you again.' I lied.

'Right, take care.' Terry winked.

He didn't need any of my help.

He was the new boy here too but he soon
had plenty of friends.

After that I saw him most Wednesdays.
We would exchange a few words in passing.
That was all. He stuck with his own kind.
There was always a group of pretty girls
at his table. I could see Terry was out
to make the most of his day at college.

2

Nina

My own course was photography.

It was something I'd always been keen on.

Even when I was quite young

I had my own camera.

I took pictures of anybody and anything;

I snapped my mates, their pets, their houses.

I took photos of nearly every street

in our town.

I liked to photograph women.

My sister Julie and her friends posed for me,

all dressed up for the disco.

'Watch out, girls.

The new David Bailey's here.'

They'd shout, then tired of posing,

Julie would say,

'Hurry up kid. We can't stand here all night.'

There was one girl on my course at college

who was really beautiful. Her name was Nina.

She was small and slim with huge dark eyes.

She had long, black hair

that hung down her back.

Nina wasn't like the other girls.

They wore scruffy jeans and baggy jumpers.

Nina always dressed in neat skirts and blouses.

In summer she wore dresses

in pale, pretty colours.

At last I found the nerve to ask Nina
if I could take some pictures of her.
To my surprise she smiled and said yes.
She stayed behind in the studio
to model for me.
I took some photos of her sitting in a chair.
They came out really well.

'They're good,' she said.
'I like them very much.'
'I really want to take some out of doors,' I said.
'Using natural light, maybe in the park.'
'OK' she said. 'How about next Saturday?
I'm not doing anything special then.
I'll meet you by the bandstand at 2 o'clock.'

3

The Perfect Model

On Saturday I was at the park much too early.

I checked the camera a dozen times.

I played about with the light meter,

and counted my spare films again and again.

I felt so nervous.

Then she came and I forgot to be shy.

She looked so beautiful.

Nina was a natural in front of the camera.

She didn't seem to notice it was there.

I took photos of her in the bandstand,

leaning against the rails.

We moved on to the children's playground

and I took a few of her sitting on a swing.

We walked down to the lake and

I took more shots.

Nina under the trees. Nina amongst the flowers.

Nina on the bridge overlooking the water.

I even asked her to get into a rowing boat.

I pushed it out a little way and she lay down.

She closed her eyes, and crossed her arms

in front of her.

With her skirt spread out and her hair

streaming around her shoulders,

she looked unreal.

Like a painting I had once seen in a book.

Time passed quickly.

'It's nearly five o'clock,' she said.

'We've been here hours.'

'It's good of you to go to all this trouble,'
I said.

She laughed.

'You don't know the half of it,' she said.

'I was scared stiff in that boat. I can't swim.
Still, all in a good cause.
You might be rich and famous one day.'

There was a little cafe at the lake side.
Over some tea she told me all about herself.
Her mother had been born in Italy.
She had died when Nina was small.

'My dad never really got over her death,
he still misses her after all this time.'

She told me her dad owned his own firm.

'He works all hours,' Nina said.

'That's why I'd better go. I like to spend some
time with him at the weekend.

Otherwise he'd be down at Brooks Yard.'

'Brooks Yard?' I said. 'Is that your dad's firm?
I had no idea. My sister Julie works there
in the office.
She's been there since she left school.'
'Is she that tall, blonde girl?' Nina asked.
'I know her. Fancy you being her brother.
It's a small world.'

I spent all of Sunday in my bedroom.
I had a small dark room in one corner.
As each photo came out
I grew more excited.
They were the best I had ever taken.

I could not wait to show the pictures to
Mr Ross, my tutor at college.
He was always keen to help.

'These are first rate,' he said on Monday.

'Mind you, you chose the perfect model.

The camera loves Nina.'

Mr Ross picked out one of her in the boat.

'I think we could improve on this,' he said.

'Fade out the hard edges.'

He showed me how to make the picture softer.

With the boat out of focus,

Nina seemed to be floating on the water.

Her long hair and the full skirt merged

with the lake,

'There you are,' Mr Ross laughed.

'The Lady of the Lake.'

4

Falling in Love

After that I saw a lot of Nina.

She would often model for me.

I must have taken hundreds of pictures of her.

We became good friends.

Nina would let me walk her home.

Sometimes she would kiss me goodnight,

but she never asked me in.

Her dad didn't like her going out with boys.

She made a joke of it.

'He doesn't think anyone's good enough
for me,' she said.

'He thinks they're after my money.'

I never thought of her as being rich
but I suppose they were pretty well off.

Their house, in its own grounds,
was very grand.

I used to leave her at the big iron gates
and watch her walk up the drive.

Then I'd go home to our little house.

Often I walked round that way again
hoping to catch a glimpse of her.

I knew I was falling in love.

One day she didn't come in to college.

I wanted to ring her, thinking she might be ill.

'The old man's off sick,' Julie told me.

'Maybe Nina's looking after him.'

The next day, in my break I went to the canteen for a cup of tea.

To my surprise I saw Nina at one of the tables. She wasn't alone.

A lad wearing a black
leather jacket was sitting next to her.
Their heads were close together.

They had their backs to me.
I stayed behind a pillar, watching.
After a while the lad got up.
He put his hand on Nina's shoulder.
She looked up, smiled and nodded.
I saw that it was Terry.
I was puzzled and as jealous as hell.
How had Nina met Terry? Not only that,
they seemed to know each other well.

I waited till he left the canteen.
Then I went over to her table.
She was staring into her empty cup.
I tried to sound casual.
'Hi, Nina.' My voice made her jump.

'Oh, hello Phil,' she said.

'I didn't see you. I was miles away.'

'Can I get you something? Another coffee?'

'No thanks,' she said. 'I have to get back.

I only came in to hand in my essay.

My dad's very ill. He's been taken to hospital.

One of the lads from the yard

is giving me a lift.'

'You don't mean Terry Barnes?' I said.

'That's right. Do you know him?'

'From way back,' I told her.

'We were at school together.

I didn't know he worked for your father,'

I said.

The idea didn't please me.

'Yes,' she said. 'He's one of dad's best workers.

Not that I know him all that well.'

She looked away.

I began to wonder how true that was.

They had seemed very friendly to me.

'I have to go,' she said. 'Terry's waiting.'

I didn't see Nina again for ages.

But I saw Terry.

In fact he came looking for me.

He handed me a key.

'Nina wants you to collect the stuff

from her locker,' he said.

'How is she?' I asked.

'Pretty low,' Terry said.

'Her dad's in a bad way.

It's his heart.'

'I'm sorry to hear that,' I said.

'I'll bring her stuff round.'

'Yeah. Sure.' Terry left in a hurry.

It would have to be him, I thought.

To be the one who's near her

at a time like this.

The one she's come to rely on.

Then I told myself to snap out of it.

I should be glad Nina had someone to

take her to the hospital.

What use would I be? I couldn't even drive.

I took her things round that night.

A woman in a black dress opened the door.

I asked to speak to Nina.

'I'm afraid you can't,' the woman said.

'She's not seeing anyone at the moment.

Her father died this afternoon.'

5

Shattered Dreams

My course was due to end in the summer.

I began looking for work.

I was lucky. I got an interview for a job

on a small local newspaper in Leeds.

I set off wearing my best suit.

The editor of the paper was a stout man

with a bald head. He had a loud voice.

He spread my photos out on his desk.

'These shots are all very well,' he said.

'But there's no call for fancy stuff here.

You'd be taking pictures of the mayor

opening the new gas works,

parties at old people's homes.

How would you cope with that kind of thing?'

'All right, I hope,' I said.

I showed him some photos

I had taken of my dad's firm,

at their annual dinner and dance.

'Just a minute,' he said. 'What's this?'

He picked out a photo of Nina

that I had taken in the park.

'Now she's one in a million,' he said.

'Is this your girlfriend?'

I had got the job.

On the train going home I was over the moon.

This job could be the start of something big.

I could go on to join a larger paper,

maybe in London.

Or even work for myself one day.

On the other hand it meant leaving my home

and family, leaving Nina.

I knew how I felt about her.

Could I ask her to wait?

There was only one way to find out.

I went straight to her house from the station.

This time she opened the door herself.

'Phil, how nice to see you. Come in,' she said.

I told her all about the interview.

How her pictures had seemed to clinch the job.

She kissed my cheek.

'I'm so pleased for you,' she said.

'I know you'll do well. You've got real talent.

Now let me tell you my good news.

Terry and I are going to be married.'

I stared at her. She went on.

'Not yet, of course.

It's too soon after dad's death.

But I'll be eighteen at the end of July

and as Terry says, "Why wait?"

He's going to help me run the firm.

My uncle wanted me to sell up

but my dad put his whole life into the business.

It's something to pass on to my own children.'

Children! I couldn't believe I was hearing this.

Nina was going to marry Terry Barnes

of all people. After all she'd meant to me.

My world seemed to fall apart.

'I wanted you to be the first to know.

You've been such a good friend,' she said.

6

Leaving

I went to the wedding.

I even took the photographs.

My present to the bride.

I tried to do a good job.

After all, I was a professional now.

Terry's mum and dad

posed with the happy couple.

They looked pleased with themselves.

They should do, I thought sourly.
Their son was getting a wonderful girl,
with a big house and a business thrown in.
No wonder he looked like the cat
that had got the cream.

I smiled afterwards when I saw how many
photos I had taken of Nina on her own.
Any excuse to leave Terry out of the picture.
He was there where it mattered most though,
in church, with Nina hanging on his arm.
Smiling up at his smug, handsome face.
You could see she was crazy about him.

Julie told me later they'd been seeing
each other for ages.
They met in secret because her dad
didn't think Terry was good enough for her.
I had to agree with him there.

I didn't think he was either.

I worked with a heavy heart on the photos.
I made my final choice for the wedding album.
Then I chose one really nice photo for myself.
The rest I stuffed into a box.
I shoved it at the back of my wardrobe
with all the others from my college days.
I would not take them with me to Leeds.
I was leaving the past behind.

7

Sad Times

It was two years before I saw Nina again.

I did not go home very often.

There was plenty to do in Leeds.

I had to find a flat, learn the job.

I passed my driving test and bought a car.

But these weren't the only reasons.

I couldn't bear the thought of seeing

Terry and Nina together.

I even made excuses not to go back for
Christmas.

Then I got a phone call from my sister, Julie.
'Mum's in hospital,' she told me.
'I think you ought to come home.
Don't worry. It's not serious
but she would like to see you.'
My boss gave me a couple of days off
and I drove home to Burford.

I went to the hospital to visit my mother.
She was pleased to see me,
but she was easily tired after her operation.
She began to nod off.
Julie said we should leave.
As we tiptoed out Julie said,
'There's someone else in here just now.'
'Who?' I asked.

'Nina. She's had an accident.'

A nurse showed me to her private room.

Nina was propped up in bed with pillows.

She lay there, staring into space.

She looked awful. I could not believe

this was the same girl who had been my model.

She had always been pale.

Now her skin was white.

Her eyes looked too big in a face

that had grown thinner.

There was a bruise on her forehead,

another on her cheek.

'Hello, Nina,' I said softly.

As she turned her head

I saw she had been crying.

She blinked as if she did not know me.

I knew I had changed quite a bit.

I was taller, not as skinny now.

My clothes were better these days.

I expect I looked quite different.

Then she smiled and I saw the old Nina.

'Phil,' she said. 'What are you doing here?'

She stretched out an arm,

and pointed to a chair.

As the sleeve fell back from her thin arm,

I saw the marks of bruises there too.

'Is it all right to stay?' I asked.

'Won't Terry be coming in to visit?'

She thought for a minute before she spoke.

'Terry can't always get away,' she said.

'He works so hard now he's running the firm.'

I didn't say anything but I felt angry.

How busy did you have to be to stay away

from a sick wife? Nina seemed in a bad way.

I began to wonder what had happened.

When I asked Julie that night she did not want

to tell me. She seemed to be holding back.

Then she said, 'OK Phil, you were bound

to find out sooner or later.

Terry hasn't been a good husband to her.

Taking over the business seems to have
gone to his head. He's really living it up.

Driving round in a flash car and so on.'

'What's all this got to do with Nina?'
I broke in.

'I'm coming to that,' Julie said.

'Now don't get mad, Phil. This is only gossip.

I don't know the whole story.

It seems Terry's been playing around.

Seeing some girl from the office.

Nina took it very badly.'

'Who wouldn't!' I shouted.

'They haven't been married long.'

Julie went on. 'Anyway, there was a row.

Terry came home very late one night.

Nina was waiting on the landing.

Her story is that she lost her balance.

She says she fell down the stairs.

She won't hear a word against him.'

I was full of anger. More than that.

I wanted to rush back to the hospital,

put my arms round Nina to comfort her.

But I knew it wasn't me she wanted.

I was glad I had seen her, one last time.

Six months later she was dead.

Drowned in her own swimming pool.

The papers said it was an accident.

There was an open verdict given

by the court. Terry was in the clear.

He had been away all day on business.

To my mind he was as guilty of her death

as if he had pushed her in himself.

I knew she had drowned herself.

Burford
Weekly
News

BROOK YARD
DAUGHTER
DROWN IN
TRAGIC
ACCIDENT

8

Revenge

I did not go to the funeral.

My next visit to Burford was for

quite a different reason.

A new club opened in the town.

The boss asked Steve Shaw,

one of our reporters, and myself

to cover the grand opening night.

The stars of one of the soaps

were all going to be there.

When we reached Burford I had time
to spare so I dropped in on Julie at work.
It was her lunch break. She had a sandwich
in one hand and a magazine in the other.
Julie was a great one for women's magazines.
She read them from cover to cover.
'Hi Phil,' she said. 'What's brought you here?'
'Where's your boss?' I asked.
The last person I wanted to see was Terry.
'It's OK. You're safe,' she said.
'He's out on business.'
We chatted for a while then I drove over
to join Steve at his hotel.

We got to the club at about nine.
There was quite a crowd outside,
waiting for the stars to arrive.
Inside it was very swish
with deep pile carpets.

There were gilt mirrors everywhere.

We moved on to the bar where

champagne was laid on for the guests.

Then we went through to the gaming room.

There were tables set up for cards

and a roulette wheel at one end

with a small crowd standing round it.

One man seemed to win quite often.

He had a glass in one hand,

and his other arm around a pretty blonde.

It was Terry Barnes.

'Black to win,' I heard his voice

before I saw his hateful face.

I wanted to go over and wipe the smile off it.

It was only a few months since Nina's death.

Steve asked the hostess to spin the wheel

while I snapped away. Then Terry saw me.

'Still working for that little rag
of a paper in Leeds, Phil,' he sneered.
'Not made it to Fleet Street yet?'
He pulled the girl closer to him
and handed her a wad of notes.
'Get me some more chips, babe.
I feel lucky tonight. Not like Phil here.
He's one of life's losers.'

I was about to take a swing at him
but Steve stepped in.
'Leave it Phil,' he said quietly. 'Let's go.
I'll give you a lift to your parents' house.'

All night I tossed and turned,
planning how to get my revenge.
In the early hours of the morning
I crept out with a box of photographs
that had been in my wardrobe all this time.
I don't know what made me do it.
It seems quite childish now.
But at the time I wasn't thinking straight.
I just wanted to punish Terry. I wanted
to remind him of what he'd done to Nina.
I drove to Brooks Yard and climbed the wall.
It was easy to break in through a small window
at the back. I was lucky there was no alarm on.

Once inside Terry's office I set to work
fixing photos of Nina to the walls.
Soon her pictures covered every inch of space.
I stuck some on the windows,
some on the filing cabinets, some on the door.
Goodness knows what I thought would happen
when Terry walked in later that morning.
Maybe I hoped he'd have a heart attack.

To this day I don't know what he thought
when he saw those rows of pictures.
The daft thing is that this stupid act
of revenge led to the big break of my life.
My career took off.
Thanks once again to Nina's photograph.

9

Still Searching

Julie told me that Terry was quite calm
when she took in his mail that morning.
He handed over the pile of photographs
he had taken down from the walls.
'I believe these belong to that idiot brother
of yours,' was all he said.

But later that day, Julie did something else.
She sorted through the photos and picked out

a dozen of the ones she liked best.

Then she sent them off to one of her

magazines.

They were holding a competition

to find a new fashion photographer.

I won first prize.

Julie came with me to London to collect it.

There was a grand meal beforehand,

laid on at a hotel in Park Lane.

Then I was given the award, together with

a cheque for one thousand pounds.

Afterwards, I had a long chat with the editor.

She asked me to join the staff of the magazine.

It was a really wonderful night

and the start of a new life for me.

I suppose in the eyes of someone like Terry

I'm a great success nowadays.

I have all the things he ever wanted:
a fancy flat in London,
the latest sports car, plenty of money.
I mix with the rich and famous, and
count models and pop stars among my friends.

My work too is always in demand.
I fly around the world
taking photographs of beautiful women.
Fashion shoots are held in exotic places:
Africa, India, the Caribbean, Bali.

But no matter where I go,
or who I happen to meet,
I'm searching for something all the time.
Something I lost along the way.
The face that still haunts my dreams.
That **one in a million**.
A girl I could love.